Fennec Finds His Voice

(Book Eleven of the Kids' Compass Series)

Fennec Finds His Voice

Written and Illustrated
by
Todd Schimmell

Art Director
Kirsten Schimmell

Copyright © 2024 by Todd Schimmell

All rights reserved. No part of this book may be reproduced or transmitted in any form or by any means, graphic, electronic, or mechanical, including photocopying, recording, taping, or by any information storage system, without the written permission of the author or publisher except in the case of brief quotations embodied in critical articles and reviews.

a Compassio Veraque LLC imprint

ISBN: 978-1-965633-97-7

printed in the United States of America

A fennec looked lost and out of place.
The desert can be a scary space.
But, there he was all alone.
This fennec was young, it was barely grown!

What was he doing? Why was he there?
A group was gathering to help and take care.

An old hyrax began to come close.
"Hello there, you seem more lost than most.
I've seen fennecs frolic near-by.
I'll help you find them, come on little guy!"

Fennec whispered, "Actually."
But the hyrax continued factually.
"I'll take you where you need to go.
Pick up your feet. You're moving too slow!"

"No silly Hyrax, let me check.
I believe he wants a ride on my neck.
He's clearly sad he's so very small.
Most animals wish to be ostrichly tall!

Climb on up Fennec, see all that I see."
Fennec sighed, "Actually…"

"Ostrich you're wrong. That's a foolish guess."
Baboon said, "He clearly needs rest."
"Actually, I was…"

"Now Fennec, I must insist you lay down.
I'll stay on guard; you can sleep safe
and sound."

"Oh come on. It doesn't need all that.
I know what it needs!" Exclaimed Polecat.

"It wants a new home, a brand-new burrow.
I'll dig one up. I'll be very thorough."

As Polecat started to dig and get dirty;
Hyrax took Fennec's paw in a hurry.

Hyrax shouted, "FOLLOW ME!"

But Ostrich scooped him up quick as can be.

Then Baboon did a ninja flip.
Snatching up Fennec with kung fu grip!

Polecat popped up from under the ground,

pulling Fennec down his burrowy mound!

Tired, Fennec tried again to speak up.
This time everyone would interupt.

All the animals jumped in and debated,
while an upset Fennec stood there and waited.

They argued, discussed, and somewhat agreed,
on exactly what Fennec would need.

"Fennec, we know what to do you see?"
"I DO NOT, ACTUALLY!!!

Thank you all for thinking and trying.
Your heart's meant well, there's no denying.
I wish you would have asked what I needed.
Is that the way you would want to be treated?

Actually, I was looking for something to eat.
A root, a fruit, or a vegetable treat."
Baboon said, "Sorry, please look by your head.
There are plenty of berries to get you fed!"

"PERFECT!
I spoke up, and you were able to help me.
Finding my voice made me
berry wealthy!"

KIDS' COMPASS QUESTIONS

1. In the beginning, were the animals able to hear what Fennec was trying to say? Why/Why Not?

2. What could the animals have done better to hear Fennec?

3. What could Fennec have done better to be heard?

When we are talking with our friends it's important to remember to listen as well. Sometimes we get too excited talking and trying to help that we forget to ask questions and truly listen.

All Todd Schimmell books are available on Amazon. Explore his other popular books like 'Boogers Are Not Food:And Other Helpful Tips', 'The Elephant Tooted', and 'Spark of Wonder:Poems to Ignite Young Imaginations'.

About The Author

Todd Schimmell "The Cartoon Cop" is a happily married father of four and an award winning school resource officer in Indiana. He welcomes reader comments on

Facebook: @authortoddschimmell

Instagram: @authortodd

www.ingramcontent.com/pod-product-compliance
Lightning Source LLC
Chambersburg PA
CBHW042127040426
42450CB00002B/100